This book belongs to

....

Dedicated to my Mum, Dad and Sister!

We started as only a family of four - who I will love and adore for evermore!!

Look how far we have come

with our growing families united as one!

Gibbs Smith and The Tennis Ball Trance

Written by Helen Smith

Illustrated by Emma Kay Smith

"TED!"

Theo shouts very **loud**
Gibbs Smith sits up tall and **proud,**
His ears start twitching, he's so delighted
Ball games make him so excited.

Ted is a cheeky little tennis ball
He know Gibbs most of all,

The Tennis Ball trance is taking hold
Time for this adventure to unfold.

Gibbs is poised as Ted launches
Ready to stand up on his haunches,

The tennis ball shoots off the racket
Gibbs Smith runs to try and catch it.

Around the garden Ted runs free
Then jumps and lands in a nearby tree,

Ted locks eyes on Gibbs to see
Yes, he's in the zone, "Gibbs follow me!"

Ted catapults around the grounds
Making some peculiar sounds,

Gibbs watches in awe as Ted takes flight

Dancing and prancing with all his might.

Quick as a flash Gibbs grabs the ball,
Making sure to break Ted's fall!

"Come on! Let's play some more."
Ted agrees. "As long as you're sure."

This little green ball has a mind of his own

Travelling without even being thrown,

This is a **Tennis Ball Trance** without a doubt
An amazing thing to shout about.

Somehow the spell needs to be **broken**
Gibbs needs to be **awoken**,

Ted knows it's time to take his leave
He's had great fun and feels really pleased.

Ted will be back another day

Creating more **mischief** is all I'll say!

As for Gibbs, I'll tell you more
He loves his new life that's for sure,
Captivating us with his happy smile
Making us go the extra mile.

Wait to see what happens next
Something that will make him flex,
What on earth could that be?
You will have to wait and see!

Gibbs Smith + family

grandm

"Gibbs Smith and the Tennis Ball Trance" is an enchanting children's book that marks the second instalment in a delightful series about a lovable dog named Gibbs. Written by Helen Smith and beautifully illustrated by Emma Kay Smith, this collaborative effort between a mother and daughter has been a labour of love spanning three years. As the story unfolds, young readers are transported into Gibbs' world, where he embarks on a thrilling adventure that involves a mysterious tennis ball. With vivid illustrations that captivate the imagination, Helen and Emma's creation captures the essence of childhood wonder and the unconditional love shared between humans and their furry friends.

Emma, the illustrator of "Gibbs Smith and the Tennis Ball Trance," has recently achieved a significant milestone in her career. After graduating from university with a degree in illustration and animation, she has transitioned into the media industry, where she now works full-time. Emma's passion for bringing stories to life through her art shines through in every vibrant and imaginative illustration she creates for the book. Meanwhile, Helen continues to make a positive impact as a teaching assistant. Her love for children and education is evident in the heartfelt and relatable stories she tells throughout the Gibbs Smith series.

In a heartfelt dedication, "Gibbs Smith and the Tennis Ball Trance" is lovingly dedicated to Helen's Mum, Dad, and Sister. It celebrates the cherished bond they share and the profound impact they have had on her life. Helen fondly reminisces about the times when it was just the four of them. From their unwavering support to the valuable lessons they've taught her, Helen owes so much to her family.

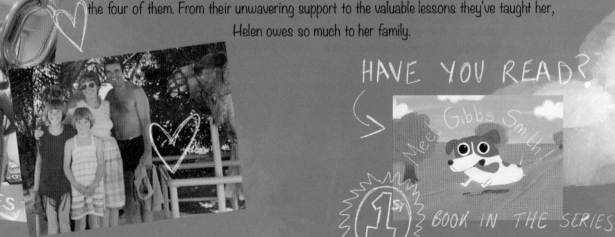

THE BURKES

HAVE YOU READ?

Meet Gibbs Smith!

1st

BOOK IN THE SERIES